Fun-Flap Facts:
Multiplication

by Danielle Blood

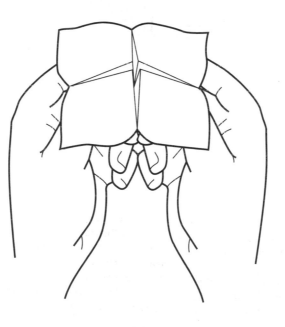

NEW YORK • TORONTO • LONDON • AUCKLAND • SYDNEY
MEXICO CITY • NEW DELHI • HONG KONG • BUENOS AIRES

SCHOLASTIC
Teaching
Resources

Fun-Flap Folding Directions

1. Trim off the top part of the fun-flap page along the solid line.

2. Place the fun-flap on a flat surface with the blank side facing up.

3. Fold back the four corners along the dotted lines so that they touch in the center of the square.

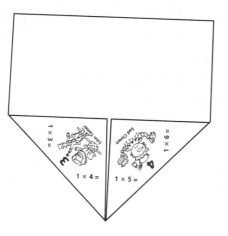

4. Turn over the fun-flap. Fold back the corners again so that they touch in the center of the square.

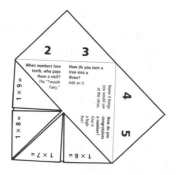

5. Fold the fun-flap in half.

6. Put your right thumb and index finger in the right side.

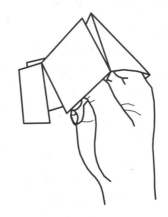

7. Put your left thumb and index finger in the left side.

8. Open and close the fun-flap by moving your fingers.

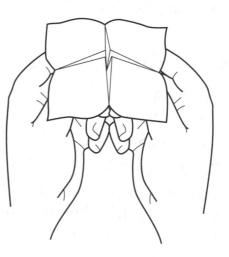

Name _____ Date _____

1. $1 \times 1 =$ _____ 1
2. $1 \times 2 =$ _____ 2
3. $1 \times 3 =$ _____ 3
4. $1 \times 4 =$ _____ 4
5. $1 \times 5 =$ _____ 5
6. $1 \times 6 =$ _____ 6
7. $1 \times 7 =$ _____ 7
8. $1 \times 8 =$ _____ 8
9. $1 \times 9 =$ _____ 9
10. $1 \times 10 =$ _____ 10
11. $1 \times 11 =$ _____ 11
12. $1 \times 12 =$ _____ 12

Name _____ Date _____

1. $2 \times 1 =$ _____ 2
2. $2 \times 2 =$ _____ 4
3. $2 \times 3 =$ _____ 6
4. $2 \times 4 =$ _____ 8
5. $2 \times 5 =$ _____ 10
6. $2 \times 6 =$ _____ 12
7. $2 \times 7 =$ _____ 14
8. $2 \times 8 =$ _____ 16
9. $2 \times 9 =$ _____ 18
10. $2 \times 10 =$ _____ 20
11. $2 \times 11 =$ _____ 22
12. $2 \times 12 =$ _____ 24

Name _____ Date _____

1. $3 \times 1 =$ _____ 3
2. $3 \times 2 =$ _____ 6
3. $3 \times 3 =$ _____ 9
4. $3 \times 4 =$ _____ 12
5. $3 \times 5 =$ _____ 15
6. $3 \times 6 =$ _____ 18
7. $3 \times 7 =$ _____ 21
8. $3 \times 8 =$ _____ 24
9. $3 \times 9 =$ _____ 27
10. $3 \times 10 =$ _____ 30
11. $3 \times 11 =$ _____ 33
12. $3 \times 12 =$ _____ 36

Name _____ Date _____

1. $4 \times 1 =$ _____ 4
2. $4 \times 2 =$ _____ 8
3. $4 \times 3 =$ _____ 12
4. $4 \times 4 =$ _____ 16
5. $4 \times 5 =$ _____ 20
6. $4 \times 6 =$ _____ 24
7. $4 \times 7 =$ _____ 28
8. $4 \times 8 =$ _____ 32
9. $4 \times 9 =$ _____ 36
10. $4 \times 10 =$ _____ 40
11. $4 \times 11 =$ _____ 44
12. $4 \times 12 =$ _____ 48

5

Name _____ Date _____

1. $5 \times 1 =$ _____ 5
2. $5 \times 2 =$ _____ 10
3. $5 \times 3 =$ _____ 15
4. $5 \times 4 =$ _____ 20
5. $5 \times 5 =$ _____ 25
6. $5 \times 6 =$ _____ 30
7. $5 \times 7 =$ _____ 35
8. $5 \times 8 =$ _____ 40
9. $5 \times 9 =$ _____ 45
10. $5 \times 10 =$ _____ 50
11. $5 \times 11 =$ _____ 55
12. $5 \times 12 =$ _____ 60

6

Name _____ Date _____

1. $6 \times 1 =$ _____ 6
2. $6 \times 2 =$ _____ 12
3. $6 \times 3 =$ _____ 18
4. $6 \times 4 =$ _____ 24
5. $6 \times 5 =$ _____ 30
6. $6 \times 6 =$ _____ 36
7. $6 \times 7 =$ _____ 42
8. $6 \times 8 =$ _____ 48
9. $6 \times 9 =$ _____ 54
10. $6 \times 10 =$ _____ 60
11. $6 \times 11 =$ _____ 66
12. $6 \times 12 =$ _____ 72

7

Name _____ Date _____

1. $7 \times 1 =$ _____ 7
2. $7 \times 2 =$ _____ 14
3. $7 \times 3 =$ _____ 21
4. $7 \times 4 =$ _____ 28
5. $7 \times 5 =$ _____ 35
6. $7 \times 6 =$ _____ 42
7. $7 \times 7 =$ _____ 49
8. $7 \times 8 =$ _____ 56
9. $7 \times 9 =$ _____ 63
10. $7 \times 10 =$ _____ 70
11. $7 \times 11 =$ _____ 77
12. $7 \times 12 =$ _____ 84

8

Name _____ Date _____

1. $8 \times 1 =$ _____ 8
2. $8 \times 2 =$ _____ 16
3. $8 \times 3 =$ _____ 24
4. $8 \times 4 =$ _____ 32
5. $8 \times 5 =$ _____ 40
6. $8 \times 6 =$ _____ 48
7. $8 \times 7 =$ _____ 56
8. $8 \times 8 =$ _____ 64
9. $8 \times 9 =$ _____ 72
10. $8 \times 10 =$ _____ 80
11. $8 \times 11 =$ _____ 88
12. $8 \times 12 =$ _____ 96

9

Name _____ Date _____

1. $9 \times 1 =$ _____ 9
2. $9 \times 2 =$ _____ 18
3. $9 \times 3 =$ _____ 27
4. $9 \times 4 =$ _____ 36
5. $9 \times 5 =$ _____ 45
6. $9 \times 6 =$ _____ 54
7. $9 \times 7 =$ _____ 63
8. $9 \times 8 =$ _____ 72
9. $9 \times 9 =$ _____ 81
10. $9 \times 10 =$ _____ 90
11. $9 \times 11 =$ _____ 99
12. $9 \times 12 =$ _____ 108

10

Name _____ Date _____

1. $10 \times 1 =$ _____ 10
2. $10 \times 2 =$ _____ 20
3. $10 \times 3 =$ _____ 30
4. $10 \times 4 =$ _____ 40
5. $10 \times 5 =$ _____ 50
6. $10 \times 6 =$ _____ 60
7. $10 \times 7 =$ _____ 70
8. $10 \times 8 =$ _____ 80
9. $10 \times 9 =$ _____ 90
10. $10 \times 10 =$ _____ 100
11. $10 \times 11 =$ _____ 110
12. $10 \times 12 =$ _____ 120

11

Name _____ Date _____

1. $11 \times 1 =$ _____ 11
2. $11 \times 2 =$ _____ 22
3. $11 \times 3 =$ _____ 33
4. $11 \times 4 =$ _____ 44
5. $11 \times 5 =$ _____ 55
6. $11 \times 6 =$ _____ 66
7. $11 \times 7 =$ _____ 77
8. $11 \times 8 =$ _____ 88
9. $11 \times 9 =$ _____ 99
10. $11 \times 10 =$ _____ 110
11. $11 \times 11 =$ _____ 121
12. $11 \times 12 =$ _____ 132

12

Name _____ Date _____

1. $12 \times 1 =$ _____ 12
2. $12 \times 2 =$ _____ 24
3. $12 \times 3 =$ _____ 36
4. $12 \times 4 =$ _____ 48
5. $12 \times 5 =$ _____ 60
6. $12 \times 6 =$ _____ 72
7. $12 \times 7 =$ _____ 84
8. $12 \times 8 =$ _____ 96
9. $12 \times 9 =$ _____ 108
10. $12 \times 10 =$ _____ 120
11. $12 \times 11 =$ _____ 132
12. $12 \times 12 =$ _____ 144

Name_____

Mark an X under "Fun-Flap Practice" after you have practiced with the fun-flap and know the facts on it. Mark an X under "Quiz" after you have taken the quiz. Record your score (how many correct out of 12).

FUN-FLAP		FUN-FLAP PRACTICE	QUIZ	QUIZ SCORE
Multiplying by 1:	Circus Time			
Multiplying by 2:	Deck of Cards			
Multiplying by 3:	Merry Monsters			
Review 1 to 3:	You're in Luck!			
Multiplying by 4:	Meet the Chicken Family			
Multiplying by 5:	Seafaring Folk			
Multiplying by 6:	One Potato, Two Potato			
Review 4 to 6:	Take a Trip			
Multiplying by 7:	Cool Postcards			
Multiplying by 8:	Super Veggies			
Multiplying by 9:	Beware of Pets			
Review 7 to 9:	Dream Career			
Multiplying by 10:	Medieval Mix-up			
Multiplying by 11:	Fantasy Vacations			
Multiplying by 12:	Nature's Wonders			
Review 10 to 12:	Extreme Sports			
Doubles:	Number Twins			
Review 2 to 12:	What a Fright!			
Review 2 to 12:	Priceless Prizes			
Review 2 to 12:	Famous Faces			
Review 2 to 12:	Folktale Folks			
Review 2 to 12:	Awesome Inventions			

Circus Time

If you joined the circus, which job would you want?

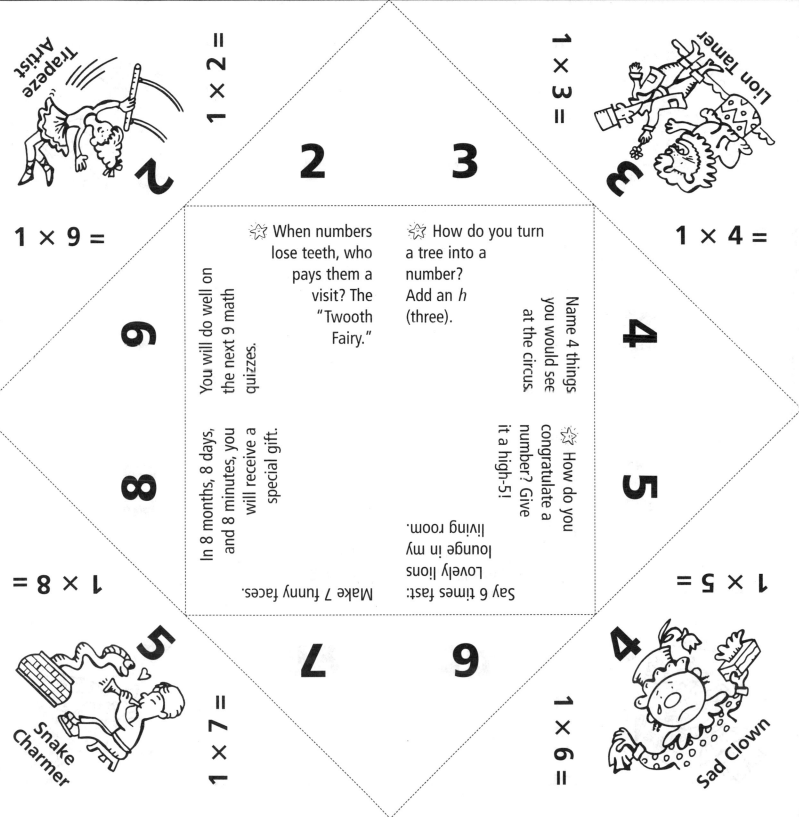

Trapeze Artist

$1 \times 2 =$

$1 \times 9 =$

2

2

Lion Tamer

$1 \times 3 =$

3

$1 \times 4 =$

3

6

9

4

8

5

When numbers lose teeth, who pays them a visit? The "Twooth Fairy."

You will do well on the next 9 math quizzes.

How do you turn a tree into a number? Add an *h* (three).

Name 4 things you would see at the circus.

How do you congratulate a number? Give it a high-5!

In 8 months, 8 days, and 8 minutes, you will receive a special gift.

Make 7 funny faces.

Say 6 times fast: Lovely lions lounge in my living room.

$1 \times 8 =$

5

Snake Charmer

$1 \times 7 =$

7

6

4

Sad Clown

$1 \times 5 =$

$1 \times 6 =$

Seafaring Folk

Whom would you pick as your tour guide of the ocean?

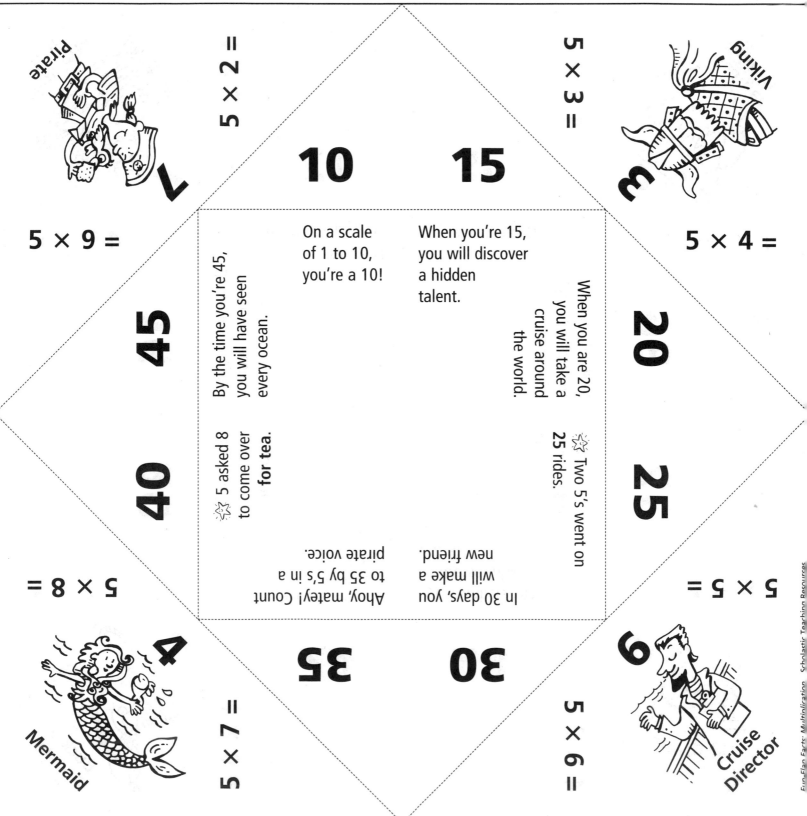

Pirate

5 × 2 =

5 × 3 =

Viking

5 × 9 =

7

10

15

3

5 × 4 =

On a scale of 1 to 10, you're a 10!

When you're 15, you will discover a hidden talent.

By the time you're 45, you will have seen every ocean.

45

When you are 20, you will take a cruise around the world.

20

☆ Two 5's went on 25 rides.

☆ 5 asked 8 to come over for tea.

40

25

5 × 8 =

Ahoy, matey! Count to 35 by 5's in a pirate voice.

In 30 days, you will make a new friend.

5 × 5 =

4

35

30

6

Mermaid

5 × 7 =

5 × 6 =

Cruise Director

One Potato, Two Potato

How do you like your potatoes?

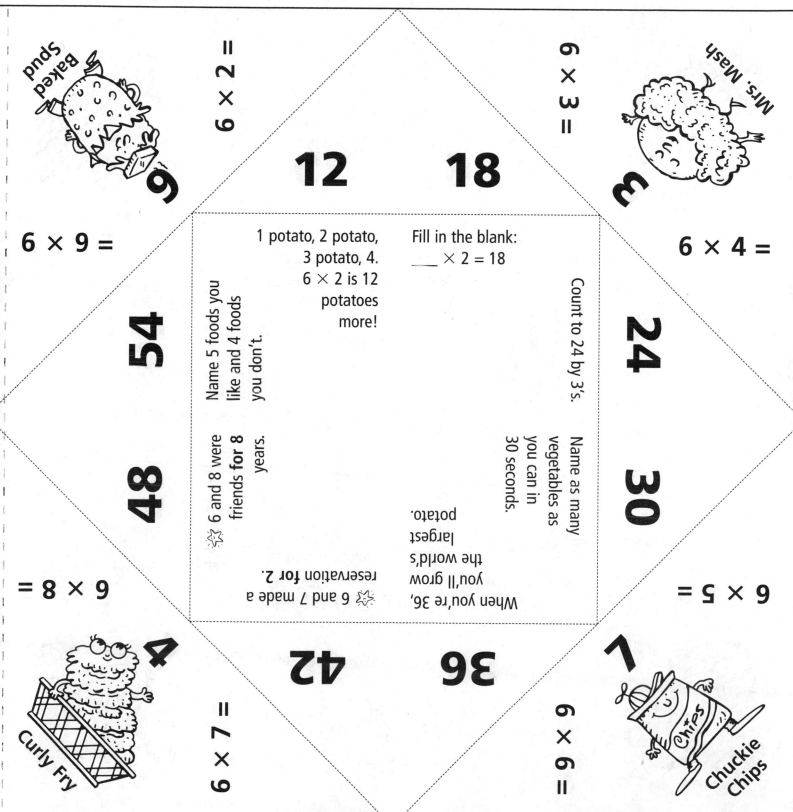

Baked Spud

$6 \times 2 =$

12

18

$6 \times 3 =$

Mrs. Mash

9

$6 \times 9 =$

3

$6 \times 4 =$

54

48

1 potato, 2 potato, 3 potato, 4. 6×2 is 12 potatoes more!

Fill in the blank:

___ $\times 2 = 18$

24

30

Name 5 foods you like and 4 foods you don't.

☆ 6 and 8 were friends **for 8** years.

Count to 24 by 3's.

Name as many vegetables as you can in 30 seconds.

$6 \times 8 =$

4

$6 \times 7 =$

42

☆ 6 and 7 made a reservation **for 2.**

When you're 36, you'll grow the world's largest potato.

36

$6 \times 5 =$

7

$6 \times 6 =$

Curly Fry

Chuckie Chips

Take a Trip

How would you like to travel?

Safari

$4 \times 9 =$

36

20

$4 \times 5 =$

Cruise

$6 \times 2 =$

$5 \times 8 =$

12

40

When you are 36, you will go on a safari.

Name as many states as you can in 20 seconds.

What do you say when 12 gets her hair cut? "Dozen it look nice?"

☆ 5 asked 8 to come over **for tea.**

36

45

When you are 36, you will become a celebrity.

Count to 45 by 5's in a baby voice.

When you are 35, you will invent a time machine.

☆ 6 and 8 were friends **for 8** years.

$6 \times 6 =$

$5 \times 9 =$

8

48

35

5

Space Voyage

$6 \times 8 =$

$5 \times 7 =$

Time Machine

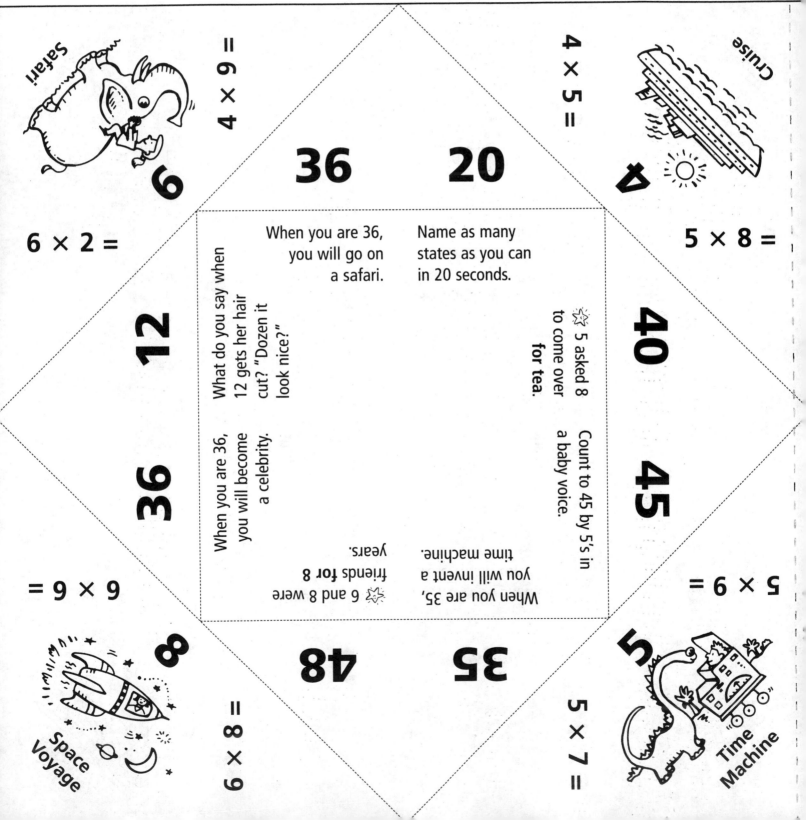

Cool Postcards

Which of these landmarks would you like to visit?

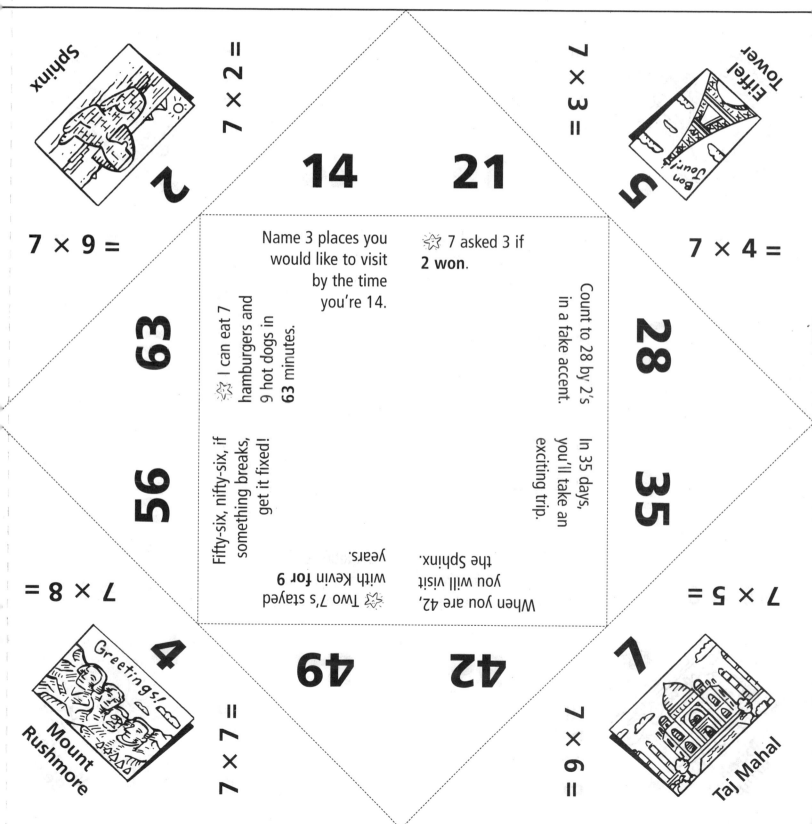

Sphinx

7 × 2 =

14 **21**

7 × 3 =

Eiffel Tower

Bon Jour!

2

7 × 9 =

7 × 4 =

Name 3 places you would like to visit by the time you're 14.

☆ 7 asked 3 if **2 won**.

☆ I can eat 7 hamburgers and 9 hot dogs in **63 minutes**.

Count to 28 by 2's in a fake accent.

63

28

In 35 days, you'll take an exciting trip.

56

35

Fifty-six, nifty-six, if something breaks, get it fixed!

☆ Two 7's stayed with Kevin for **9** years.

When you are 42, you will visit the Sphinx.

7 × 8 =

4

7 × 7 =

49 **42**

7 × 5 =

7

Mount Rushmore

Greetings!

7 × 6 =

Taj Mahal

Dream Career

What's your dream career?

Astronaut

$7 \times 9 =$

63

35

Rock Star

$7 \times 5 =$

8

$9 \times 2 =$

☆ I can eat 7 hot dogs and 9 hamburgers in **63** minutes.

When you are 35, your dream career will come true!

$8 \times 8 =$

18

Count backward from 18 by 2's.

☆ 8 asked 8, "What did you yell at **6 for?**"

64

54

Fifty-four, nifty-four, always knock before opening a door.

Name as many jobs as you can in 32 seconds.

32

In 27 days, you will discover a cool secret.

Fill in the blank: $56 + \underline{\hspace{1cm}} = 100$

$9 \times 6 =$

President

5

27

56

Detective

3

$9 \times 3 =$

$8 \times 7 =$

$8 \times 4 =$

Medieval Mix-up

Who's your favorite character?

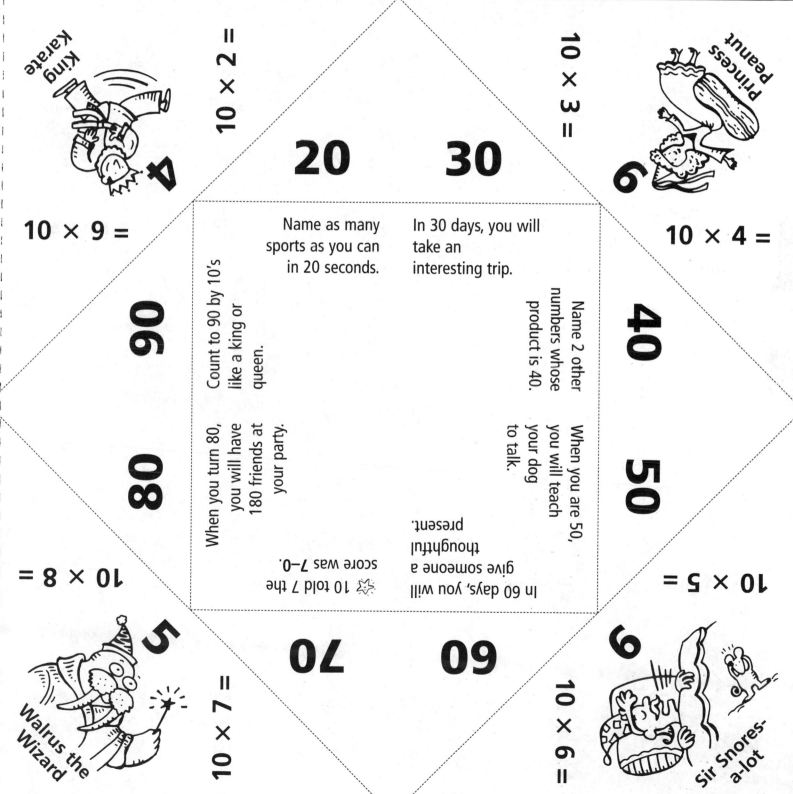

King Karate

$10 \times 2 =$

$10 \times 3 =$

Princess Peanut

4

20

30

6

$10 \times 9 =$

Name as many sports as you can in 20 seconds.

In 30 days, you will take an interesting trip.

$10 \times 4 =$

90

Count to 90 by 10's like a king or queen.

Name 2 other numbers whose product is 40.

40

80

When you turn 80, you will have 180 friends at your party.

When you are 50, you will teach your dog to talk.

50

In 60 days, you will give someone a thoughtful present.

★ 10 told 7 the score was 7–0.

$10 \times 8 =$

5

70

60

6

$10 \times 5 =$

Walrus the Wizard

$10 \times 7 =$

$10 \times 6 =$

Sir Snores-a-lot

Fantasy Vacations

If you could visit one of these places, which would it be?

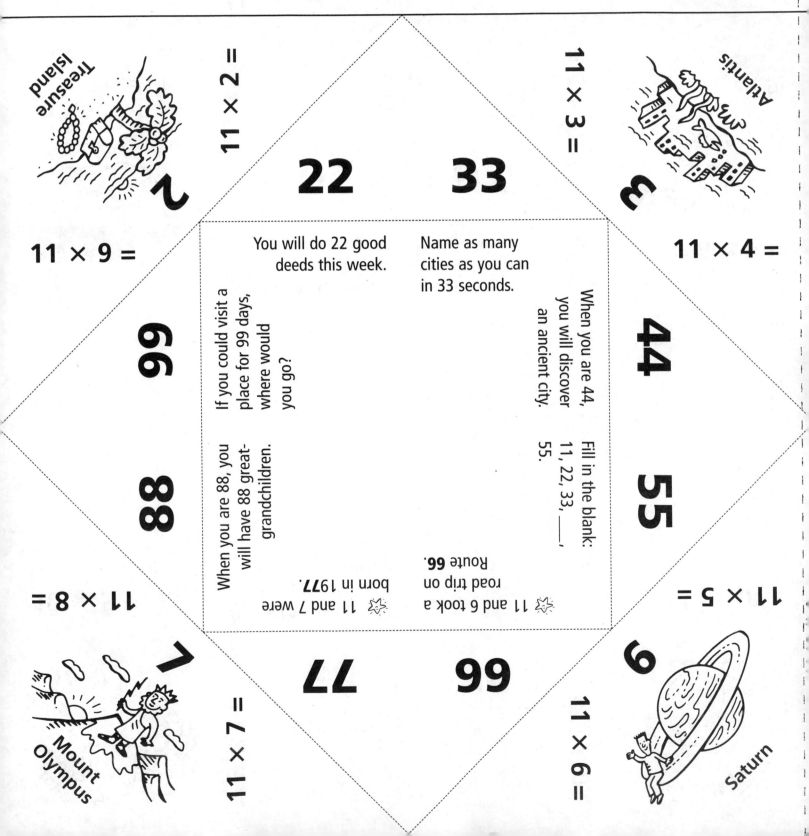

Treasure Island

$11 \times 2 =$

2

$11 \times 9 =$

22

33

$11 \times 3 =$

Atlantis

3

$11 \times 4 =$

You will do 22 good deeds this week.

Name as many cities as you can in 33 seconds.

If you could visit a place for 99 days, where would you go?

When you are 44, you will discover an ancient city.

Fill in the blank: 11, 22, 33, ____, 55.

99

44

When you are 88, you will have 88 great-grandchildren.

88

55

☆ 11 and 6 took a road trip on Route 66.

☆ 11 and 7 were born in 1977.

$11 \times 8 =$

7

$11 \times 7 =$

77

66

$11 \times 5 =$

6

$11 \times 6 =$

Mount Olympus

Saturn

Nature's Wonders

Which of these things would you like to be an expert on?

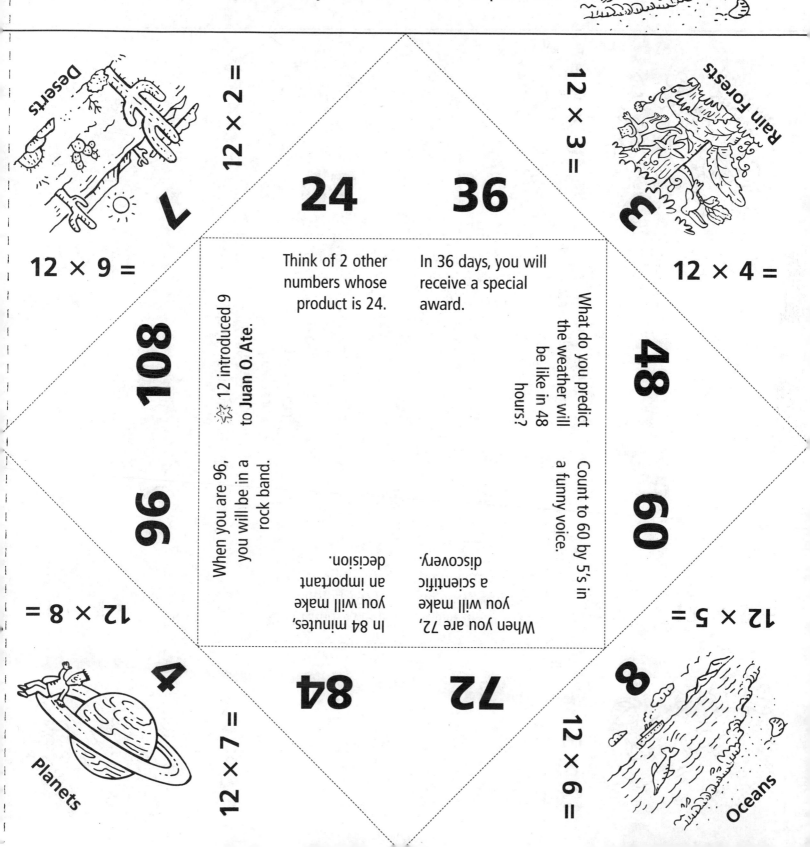

Deserts

$12 \times 2 =$

Rain Forests

$12 \times 9 =$

7

24

36

3

$12 \times 3 =$

$12 \times 4 =$

108

☆ 12 introduced 9 to **Juan O. Ate.**

Think of 2 other numbers whose product is 24.

In 36 days, you will receive a special award.

What do you predict the weather will be like in 48 hours?

48

96

When you are 96, you will be in a rock band.

Count to 60 by 5's in a funny voice.

60

$12 \times 8 =$

4

In 84 minutes, you will make an important decision.

When you are 72, you will make a scientific discovery.

$12 \times 5 =$

8

Planets

$12 \times 7 =$

84

72

$12 \times 6 =$

Oceans

Extreme Sports

Which extreme sport would you like to try someday?

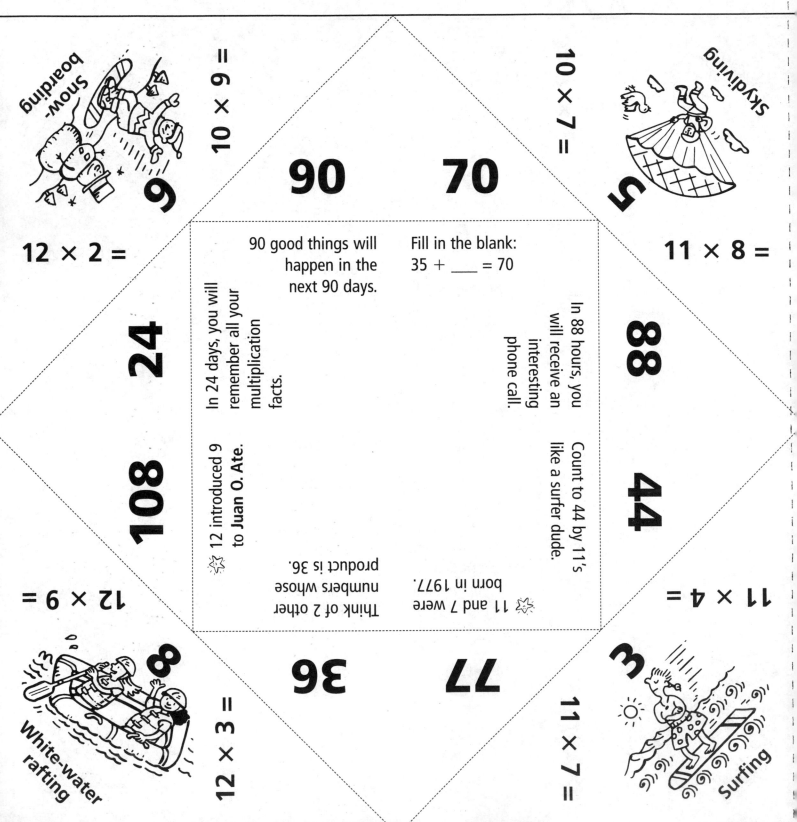

Snow-boarding

$10 \times 9 =$

Skydiving

$10 \times 7 =$

90 **70**

9

5

$12 \times 2 =$

$11 \times 8 =$

90 good things will happen in the next 90 days.

Fill in the blank:
$35 +$ ___ $= 70$

24

In 24 days, you will remember all your multiplication facts.

In 88 hours, you will receive an interesting phone call.

88

108

☆ 12 introduced 9 to Juan O. Ate.

Count to 44 by 11's like a surfer dude.

44

$12 \times 9 =$

Think of 2 other numbers whose product is 36.

☆ 11 and 7 were born in 1977.

$11 \times 4 =$

8

36 **77**

3

White-water rafting

$12 \times 3 =$

$11 \times 7 =$

Surfing

Number Twins

Pick your favorite pair of twins.

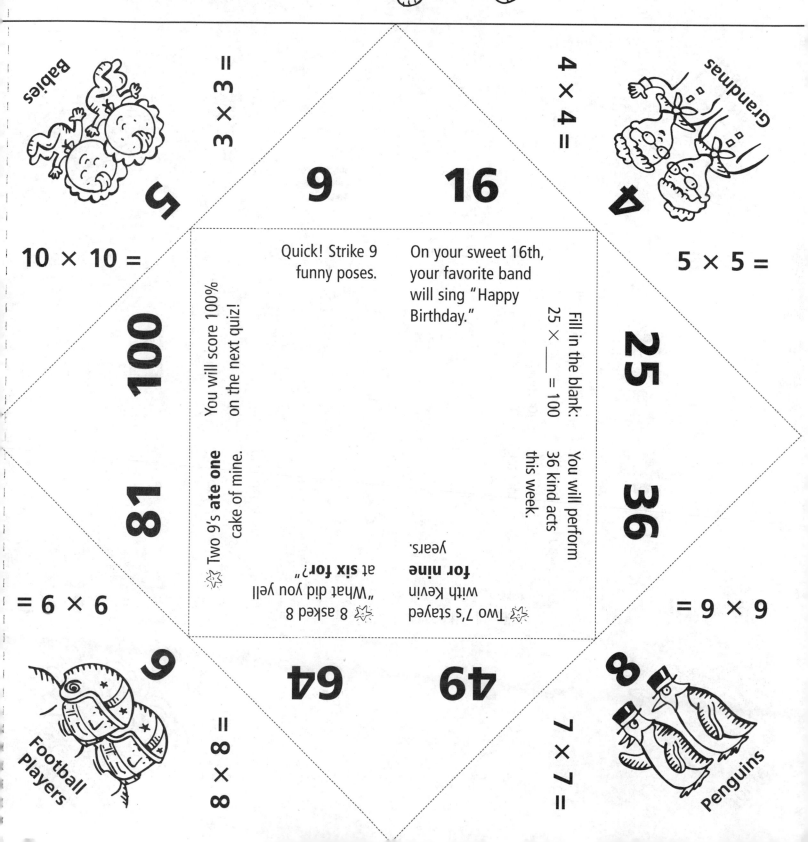

Babies

$3 \times 3 =$

9   **16**

$4 \times 4 =$

Grandmas

$10 \times 10 =$

5 × 5 =

You will score 100% on the next quiz!

100

Quick! Strike 9 funny poses.

On your sweet 16th, your favorite band will sing "Happy Birthday."

Fill in the blank: $25 \times \underline{\quad} = 100$

You will perform 36 kind acts this week.

25

81

Two 9's **ate one** cake of mine.

36

$6 \times 6 =$

$9 \times 9 =$

Two 7's stayed with Kevin **for nine** years.

8 asked 8 "What did you yell **at six for?**"

9

64

49

8

Football Players

$8 \times 8 =$

$7 \times 7 =$

Penguins

What a Fright!

Who's the scariest of them all?

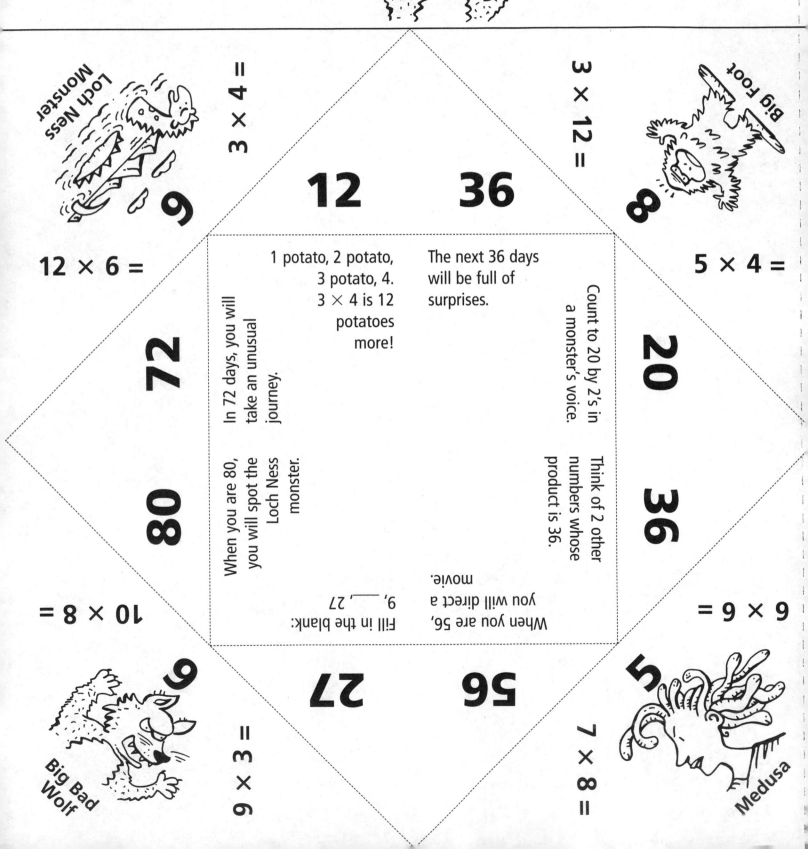

Loch Ness Monster

Big Foot

$3 \times 4 =$

$3 \times 12 =$

12

36

$12 \times 6 =$

$5 \times 4 =$

72

20

1 potato, 2 potato, 3 potato, 4. 3×4 is 12 potatoes more!

The next 36 days will be full of surprises.

In 72 days, you will take an unusual journey.

Count to 20 by 2's in a monster's voice.

80

36

When you are 80, you will spot the Loch Ness monster.

Think of 2 other numbers whose product is 36.

When you are 56, you will direct a movie.

Fill in the blank: 9, ____, 27

$10 \times 8 =$

$6 \times 6 =$

9

27

56

5

$9 \times 3 =$

$7 \times 8 =$

Big Bad Wolf

Medusa

Priceless Prizes

You're the lucky winner! Pick a prize.

Chocolate

Hope Diamond

$2 \times 9 =$

$4 \times 6 =$

Winning Raffle Ticket

4

18

24

8

$11 \times 9 =$

The 18th will be your lucky day in school.

Think of 2 other numbers whose product is 24.

$4 \times 4 =$

Think of 2 numbers whose sum is 16.

99

You will win a contest in 99 days.

16

Name 4 prizes you'd like to win and 2 you wouldn't.

84

42

In 84 minutes, you'll learn something very interesting.

☆ I can eat 9 hot dogs and 7 hamburgers in **63** minutes.

☆ Two 7's stayed with Kevin for **nine** years.

$12 \times 7 =$

3

63

49

6

Lifetime Supply of Chocolate

$9 \times 7 =$

$7 \times 7 =$

No More Homework

$6 \times 7 =$

Bon Voyage

Famous Faces

Whom would you like to interview?

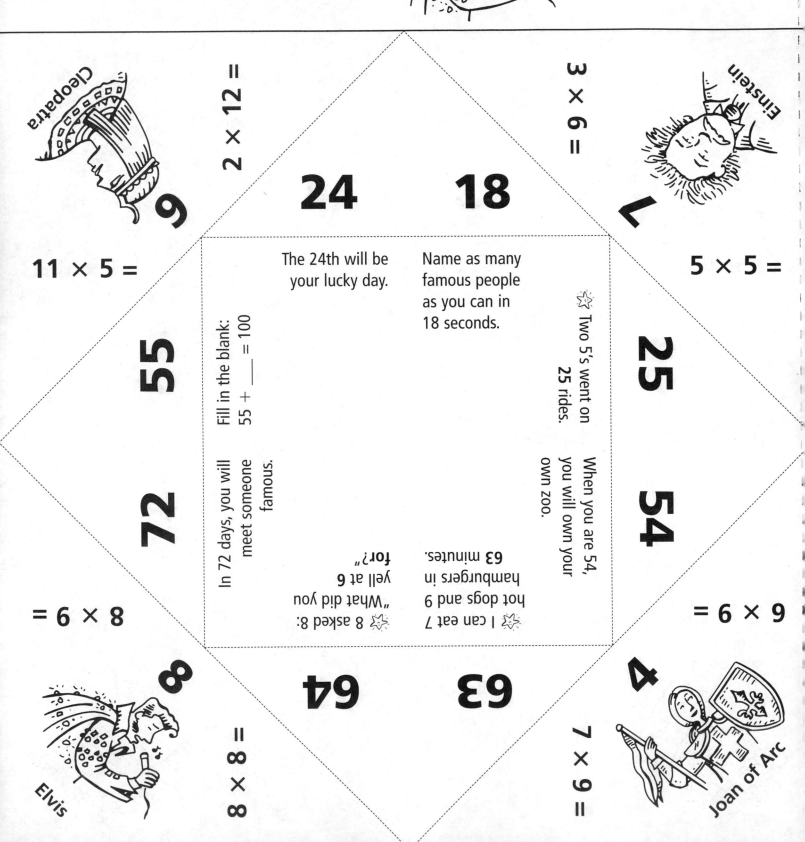

Cleopatra

$2 \times 12 =$

$3 \times 6 =$

Einstein

9

24

18

7

$11 \times 5 =$

$5 \times 5 =$

The 24th will be your lucky day.

Name as many famous people as you can in 18 seconds.

☆ Two 5's went on 25 rides.

55

25

Fill in the blank: $55 + \underline{} = 100$

When you are 54, you will own your own zoo.

72

54

In 72 days, you will meet someone famous.

☆ 8 asked 8: "What did you yell at 6 for?"

☆ I can eat 7 hot dogs and 9 hamburgers in 63 minutes.

Elvis

$8 \times 9 =$

$6 \times 9 =$

Joan of Arc

8

64

63

4

$8 \times 8 =$

$7 \times 9 =$

Folktale Folks

Who's your favorite folktale character?

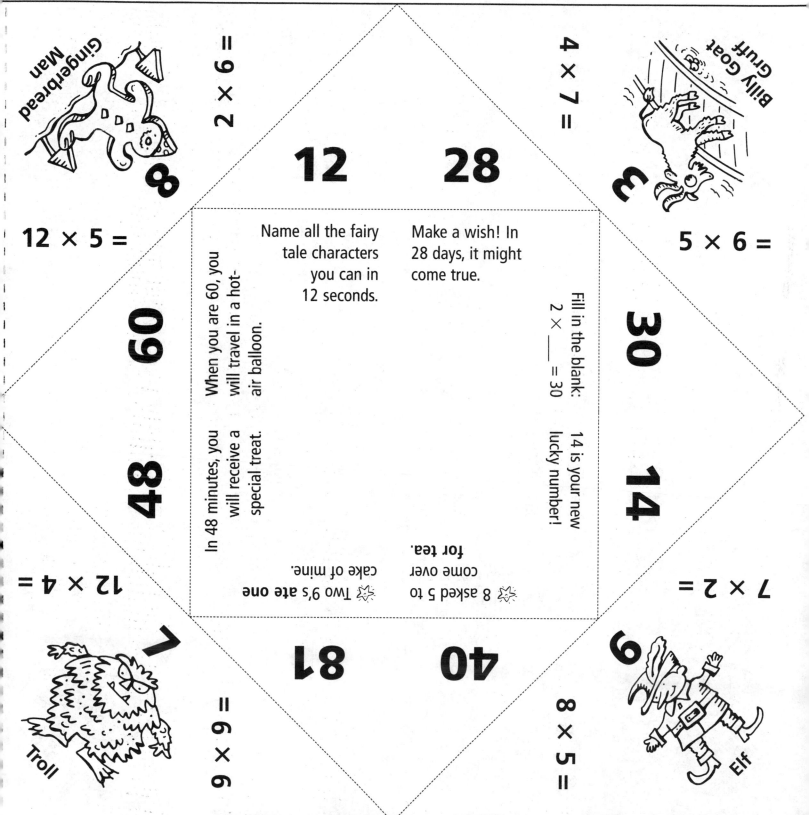

Gingerbread Man

8

$2 \times 6 =$

$12 \times 5 =$

12

28

Billy Goat Gruff

3

$4 \times 7 =$

$5 \times 6 =$

Name all the fairy tale characters you can in 12 seconds.

Make a wish! In 28 days, it might come true.

When you are 60, you will travel in a hot-air balloon.

In 48 minutes, you will receive a special treat.

Fill in the blank:
$2 \times \underline{\quad} = 30$

14 is your new lucky number!

60

48

30

14

☆ Two 9's ate one cake of mine.

☆ 8 asked 5 to come over for tea.

Troll

7

$12 \times 4 =$

$9 \times 9 =$

81

40

Elf

9

$7 \times 2 =$

$8 \times 5 =$

Awesome Inventions

Which one would you like to invent?

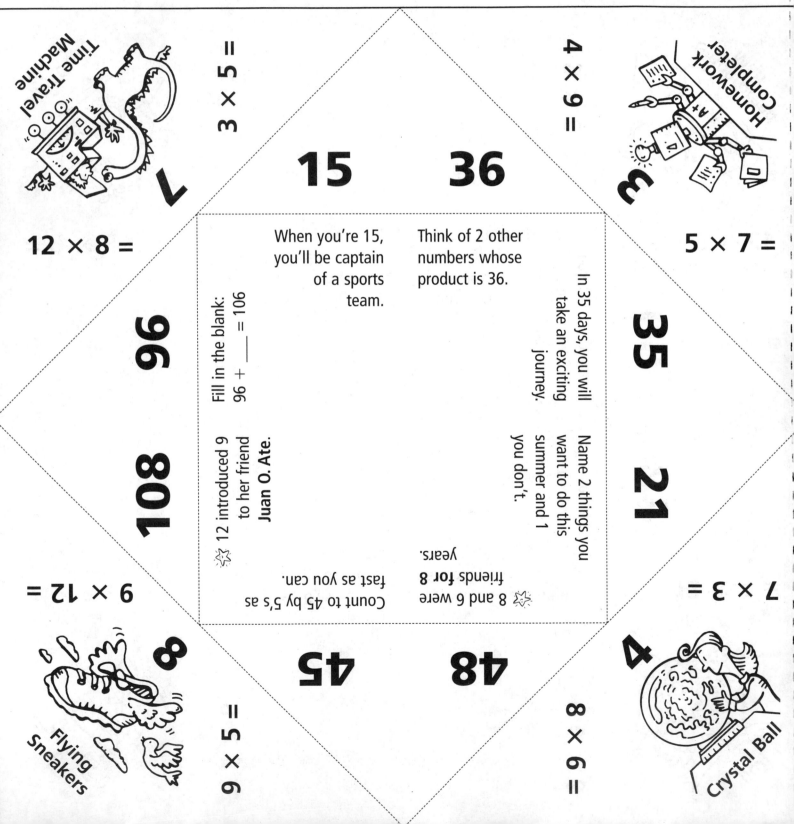

Time Travel Machine

7

$3 \times 5 =$

15

36

$4 \times 9 =$

Homework Completer

3

$12 \times 8 =$

$5 \times 7 =$

96

Fill in the blank:
$96 + \underline{\hspace{1cm}} = 106$

When you're 15, you'll be captain of a sports team.

Think of 2 other numbers whose product is 36.

In 35 days, you will take an exciting journey.

35

108

☆ 12 introduced 9 to her friend **Juan O. Ate.**

Name 2 things you want to do this summer and 1 you don't.

21

$9 \times 12 =$

8

Count to 45 by 5's as fast as you can.

☆ 8 and 6 were friends **for 8** years.

$7 \times 3 =$

4

Flying Sneakers

$9 \times 5 =$

45

48

$8 \times 6 =$

Crystal Ball